Where Is the Image of God in You?
Expressing Character Traits in Godly Ways

Group Member's Guide

By: Brad Rymer

Communications should be addressed to:
Living Free Ministries, Inc.
P. O. Box 22127
Chattanooga, TN 37422-2127

Persons identified as having specific character traits represent a composite of the author's counseling experience, and no one individual is portrayed in this volume.

Unless otherwise indicated, Scripture quotations are taken from the Holy Bible, New Living Translation, Copyright ©1996. Used by permission of Tyndale House Publishers, Wheaton, Illinois 60189. All rights reserved. Other Scripture quotations marked KJV are from the King James Version of the Bible. Those identified NIV are from the Holy Bible, New International Version, Copyright ©1973, 1978, 1984, International Bible Society. The Scripture quotations marked THE MESSAGE are taken from The Message, Copyright ©1993, 1994, 1995, 1996, 2000, 2001, 2002. Used by permission of NavPress Publishing Group.

©Living Free Ministries, 2010. All rights reserved.

All rights are reserved. No part of the material protected by this copyright notice may be reproduced or utilized in any form or by any means, electronic or mechanical, including photocopying, recording, or any information storage and retrieval system without written permission from the Living Free Ministries.

ISBN 978-1-58119-113-4

Discovering God's Path to Freedom

Cover: Linda Miller
Arnold Miller Promotions
Phone: 423-263-4900
www.arnoldmiller.com

Layout: Louise Lee

About the Author

Brad Rymer is actively involved in leading Living Free groups and serves on the Living Free board of directors. He and his wife, Babs, co-chaired the *Living Free* video project.

Trained in conflict mediation at the Institute for Christian Conciliation (a division of Peacemaker® Ministries), Brad is a marriage and family mediator. He coordinated the small group project on peacemaking with Peacemaker® Ministries and Living Free Ministries. He also served as editor of the *Peacemaking* small group curriculum.

Brad was the recepient of the 2010 Living Free Distinguished Ministry Award. This award is given for outstanding dedication and leadership.

Where Is the Image of God in You?

Contents

	Page
Preface	i
Character Trait Chart	ii
Orientation	1
Session 1 — The Image of God in You—Relating to Perfection	6
Session 2 — The Image of God in You—Relating to Performance	11
Session 3 — The Image of God in You—Relating to Pleasure	17
Session 4 — The Image of God in You—Relating to Determination	22
Session 5 — The Image of God in You—Relating to Servanthood	28
Session 6 — The Image of God in You—Relating to Passion	34
Session 7 — The Image of God in You—Relating to Inquiry	41
Session 8 — The Image of God in You—Relating to Examination	50
Session 9 — The Image of God in You—Relating to Peacefulness	56
Session 10 — The Image of God in You—Relating to Your Neighbor	63
Session 11 — The Image of God in You—Relating to Your Family	71
Session 12 — The Image of God in You—Relating to Your Spouse and God	76
Plan of Salvation	82
References	83

Preface
Where Is the Image of God in You?

The purpose of this study is for us to see how some of the different character traits we have can be used in constructive rather than destructive ways in our lives and relationships so that we are operating more and more in the image of God according to the way He created us. Also, this study can help us better understand others as we build godly relationships.

We were created in the image of God which is found in man's personality, intelligence, moral responsibility, and knowledge. We have the capacity to think, make decisions, reason and show emotion, exercise knowledge, have moral or immoral character, and have dominion over the earth. "The biblical view is that man is made to know God as well as to obey him" (Elwell, 547). The fall of man did not destroy the image but marred it. Through Jesus Christ, the divine image is restored (Ephesians 4:24).

Being made in the image of God, we are called to do the will of God. Jesus showed us the way. "He showed us how in choosing and doing the will of God, and making it his own will" (Murray, 127). Jesus said, "I have come to do your will, O God" (Hebrews 10:7).

To be like Jesus means the pursuit of a holy life. He is described as "the Holy One of God" (John 6:69). "God is morally spotless in character and action, upright, pure and untainted with evil desires, motives, thought, words, or acts" (Elwell, 455). As we know and obey our Lord, we will "be conformed to the likeness of his Son" (Romans 8:29 NIV).

We will also explore the love of God as it relates to our character traits. We will look at why God loves us and how He helps us love others. "See how very much our heavenly father loves us, for he allows us to be called his children, and we really are" (1 John 3:1)!

On the following page is a list of common character traits we will explore. The traits are described in negative and positive terms. From a biblical perspective, we would refer to using these character traits in a worldly way or a godly way: operating in the flesh (the sin nature) versus operating in the Spirit, being self-centered or God-centered and others-centered, or acting in unloving ways or loving ways. Each of the character trait descriptions will be referred to as: "Seems Natural, Makes Life Hard" and "Seems Hard, Makes Life Good." These character traits are by no means all of God's or mankind's traits. Some participants may identify with one or more while others may not identify very strongly with any but can learn to relate to and help others. This study represents some of the character traits and related issues observed in people.

This group material is not designed to be an exhaustive study of the image of God. Instead, our goal is to help each participant understand that God has a divine design for our lives. We will look at various character traits that can help us express some selected character traits in a godly way.

Finally, if you have not received Christ as your Savior, you are invited to make this important decision (see page 82). May God bless you abundantly as you are guided by His Word to do His will and live a holy life.

Group Member's Guide: *Where Is the Image of God in You?*, Living Free, P. O. Box 22127, Chattanooga, TN 37422-2127

Character Trait Chart

CHARACTER TRAIT	SEEMS NATURAL, MAKES LIFE HARD	SEEMS HARD, MAKES LIFE GOOD
Perfection	I tend to focus on judging and criticizing what is wrong with me and others more than on what is right and positive.	I choose to focus on loving what is right and good about myself, others, and life rather than dwelling on what I view as wrong.
Performance	I strive to accomplish many things each day in order to feel a sense of value and worth.	I can find comfort and rest in knowing that who I am is more important than what I can do. I accept that despite my weaknesses and failures, I am loved.
Pleasure	Give me more, more, more. "Eat, drink, and be merry, for tomorrow we may die." In pursuing mostly fun activities, I try to avoid trudging through the harder parts of life.	I am willing to accept the bad with the good. I appreciate balance and moderation. I enjoy seasons of pleasure, not pleasure as all there is to this life.
Determination	When I do not agree with, like, or think it is fair the way things are being done, I feel compelled to take charge immediately.	I will choose my battles wisely. While being bold to stand against what I believe to be wrong and stand for what I think is right, I will control my anger and consider God and others in my approach.
Servanthood	I am compelled to be helpful to others in a way that makes me feel good. I often prefer to please someone rather than consider if what they want is reasonable or wise.	I will move in and out of others' lives according to what is best, wise, and healthy, not solely on what I or they desire.
Passion	I allow my emotions to rule my actions and perspectives of my relationships and circumstances.	I love the beauty in the world and appreciate the richness of the relationships and blessings I have.
Inquiry	I am fearful and doubtful of many things in life. I sense there is much to question in order to find assurance.	Because of my faith in God, I can grow in trust and confidence that I am secure in His plan for my life.
Examination	If I can gather enough information and be left alone long enough to examine it, I can work out any problem in life.	I will defer to God's wisdom to know when to share my thoughts and needs with others as it is through others that God often meets our needs.
Peacefulness	I try to be or appear to be pleasing, agreeable, and accepting of everyone in order to maintain peace and harmony.	I will engage in relationships in a way that allows for honest, caring, and patient communication as well as trusting in God to bring about peace beyond my capabilities.

Orientation

Personal Preparation: Getting Ready for Orientation

So God created man in his own image (Genesis 1:27a, NIV).

Welcome

Personal Notes

Welcome to the *Where Is the Image of God in You? Group*. You have taken a positive step. We thank God for your participation.

During this course, there will be suggested time alone with God in meditation, prayer, and scripture reading. This time is vital as we look at character traits. We encourage you to be faithful in your devotion time with the Lord.

> A character trait is a distinguishing quality or attribute notable to a person.

For this session, read Psalm 139.

As a starter for this course, briefly share your name and what you are interested in about this course and state one thing about yourself that pleases you and one thing about yourself that frustrates you.

Group Member's Guide: *Where Is the Image of God in You?*, Living Free, P. O. Box 22127, Chattanooga, TN 37422-2127

Self-Awareness

You are about to take a journey in finding truths about yourself, God, and others.

As human beings, we have many things in common; and yet we are totally unique! This course is designed for us to see how some of the different character traits we have can be used in constructive rather than destructive ways in our lives and relationships so that we are operating more and more in the image of God according to the way He created us. In other words, our goal will be to express our character traits in ways which help us "become like his Son" (Romans 8:29).

In Rymer's experience as a marriage and family counselor, he has noticed things people want to change about themselves and others which reveal different character traits they are focused on. For instance, if someone complains: "My husband will never admit to being wrong," and the husband says: "That's because I am always right," it appears the husband has some level of focus on the character trait Perfection—a desire for self and others to be and do things the right way. The problem comes in determining by whose definition we determine "the right way."

Starting with Perfection, we will look at one character trait per session. We will explore how to view each trait biblically as being used either from a worldly perspective or from a godly perspective. This depends on our motives, attitudes, and points of view.

You may discover that you operate primarily around one or more of the principles described in one of these traits, or you may not see yourself in one of these common traits, but you can learn how to better relate to others. An understanding of all of these traits will help you see more clearly what you share in common with others and how you are different. Additionally, we will discuss ways to develop the godly nature of these traits while ridding ourselves of the negative aspects. (See the Preface of this study guide for a summary of some of the negative and positive ways to operate out of these traits).

The group member's guide is designed to prepare each participant for the group meeting.

2 Orientation Group Member's Guide: *Where Is the Image of God in You?*, Living Free, P. O. Box 22127, Chattanooga, TN 37422-2127

Although there are other character traits, we will focus on the following:

PERFECTION	**DETERMINATION**	**INQUIRY**
PERFORMANCE	**SERVANTHOOD**	**EXAMINATION**
PLEASURE	**PASSION**	**PEACEFULNESS**

Pick a trait mentioned and describe ways you personally display an aspect of the trait negatively and positively—in an ungodly way or a godly way.

A common question couples in counseling ask is: "Can you help us communicate better?"

Some communication improvement can be made when we begin to realize none of the character traits such as these we will study are right or wrong or better or worse than the others. They are all different, and each of us has our own unique expression of the traits we hold dearest.

So how do we express these traits in a way that brings God's will to our lives and relationships? That will be the focus of our study.

How can we best know who we really are? God created us, so perhaps it is best to learn more about the nature of God and His plan. First, we see that we can be holy because God is holy. "Be holy because I, the LORD your God, am holy (Leviticus 19:2). Holiness is an outflow of God's nature.

Ephesians 1:4 states: "Long ago, even before he made the world, God loved us and chose us in Christ to be holy and without fault in his eyes."

What does this say about God?

What does this say about us as human beings?

What does this say about you?

Spiritual-Awareness

Man was created God-like; he was made like God in character and personality. And throughout the Scriptures the standard and goal set before man is to be like God. Leviticus 19:2; Matthew 5:45-48; Ephesians 5:1. And to be like God means to be like Christ, who is the image of the invisible God (Pearlman, 115).

1 John 4:16-17

In these verses we see that "God is love." The more we learn about and believe this aspect of God, the more we will appreciate how He has made us. In Ephesians 1:4, we see that God loves us.

What do you think is the connection between love and trust?

What is the difference between "perfect love" and imperfect love?

What is the connection between perfect love and fear?

According to verse 16, how close can we be to God?

Zephaniah 3:17b

This verse gives us a delightful picture of just how much God loves us.

What does this verse say God will do for us with His love?

Application

As we explore aspects of the character traits, we will always bring our focus back to God's holiness and His love. With His love and by following His will, we can operate in healthy and positive ways. Without His love and guidance, we will use these traits in negative and destructive ways.

Looking again at 1 John 4:17, we see that our focusing more on love is a process: "Our love grows more perfect." This is a growth process—becoming like Christ.

Name some ways you think you can walk in God's holiness and be more loving in light of God's love in one or more of the character traits listed in the Self-Awareness portion of this session.

God loves us so much that He sent His only son.
　　For God so loved the world that he gave his only Son, so that everyone who believes in him will not perish but have eternal life. God did not send his Son into the world to condemn it, but to save it (John 3:16-17).

In John 14:6, God displays His love for us by showing the way to himself is through His Son. "Jesus told him, 'I am the way, the truth, and the life. No one can come to the Father except through me.'"

Our goal in this study is to follow God's will and be like him as we develop the various character traits in our lives.

Session 1: The Image of God in You—Relating to Perfection

Personal Preparation: Getting Ready for Session One

But you are to be perfect, even as your Father in heaven is perfect (Matthew 5:48).

Meet with God

Personal Notes

Take 30 minutes each day to be alone with God in meditation and prayer. Read 2 Peter 1.

May the next few weeks be a time of encouragement for you.

Describe a time when you were frustrated with yourself for not doing something just right or "to perfection."

Self-Awareness

Character Trait	Seems Natural, Makes Life Hard	Seems Hard, Makes Life Good
Perfection	I tend to focus on judging and criticizing what is wrong with me and others more than on what is right and positive.	I choose to focus on loving what is right and good about myself, others, and life rather than dwelling on what I view as wrong.

Long before Rymer became a marriage counselor or studied character traits, someone said something in a conversation he has never forgotten. It was one of those "talking-about-nothing-in-particular" exchanges when a co-worker announced rather emphatically: "I realize there is more than one way to do things, my way or the wrong way!" If you strongly identify with this comment or suddenly are asking yourself if that person could have been you, perfection is something you probably focus on.

In sessions 1-9, we will look at some of the different character traits we have. When we can identify the ways we use and focus on different character traits, it will help us understand why we see and do things the way we do. It will also give us a greater understanding of others as we begin to understand and appreciate the traits they focus on. This understanding will lead to improved communication with others which leads to better relationships, the ultimate goal of this process.

This session deals with the first trait we will discuss: **Perfection**. As we go through each trait, reflect on how you relate and display or do not relate strongly with each one. Also, make an effort to understand and appreciate why others focus the way they do on each of the traits.

Striving for perfection solely by human effort can be a very frustrating endeavor. We tend to load ourselves down with "shoulds." "I should do this or that; I should have done it this way; I should read my Bible more; I should be more loving." We can also project this focus onto others: "He should be more sensitive; she should be more respectful; they should be more open; that person should pay more attention to how they are driving, etc."

Name one of your "pet peeves" regarding things people do or circumstances that frustrate you.

You can probably see that when your focus is on human perfection, many things can frustrate you. Frustration can build into resentment. Resentment can build into a critical and judgmental attitude towards self and others. This attitude can lead to bitterness and unforgiveness—not a pretty picture.

So we turn our focus back to love. In the Spiritual Awareness portion of this session, let's look at perfection from a biblical perspective.

Life has perfect moments—"But you are to be perfect, even as your Father in heaven is perfect" (Matthew 5:48).

Perfection comes naturally to God. Maybe you have noticed it does not come naturally to us. Therefore, we have to be intentional about perfection. But how do we follow this command? It begins with perfect moments. When I choose to respond to any given person or circumstance in a godly way, I have just had a perfect moment and therefore have fulfilled this command—in that moment.

Describe a time when, maybe even against the way you felt, you handled a situation in a godly, loving way and you had "a perfect moment."

Spiritual-Awareness

As we discuss perfection, we are reminded of our holy Savior. "For God made Christ, who never sinned, to be the offering for our sin, so that we could be made right with God through Christ" (2 Corinthians 5:21).

2 Peter 1:3-4

In these verses we see where the "power" comes from to have "perfect moments." Remember, worldly perfection is focused more on being right and godly perfection is based on being holy and loving. Godly perfection does not come naturally to us.

By whose nature or power does verse 3 say we can live a godly life?

Verse 4 says by sharing in His [Jesus'] divine nature, we escape the problems caused by evil desires.

Being right is not necessarily a bad thing.

Describe what happens, however, when being right is placed above being loving.

How does this lead to a form of corruption described in this verse?

Hebrews 12:1-3 NIV

The Bible refers to Jesus as the "author and perfecter" of our faith and instructs us to "fix our eyes on Jesus" (v2).

From these passages, describe the difference between viewing perfection from a worldly perspective and viewing perfection from a biblical perspective.

Matthew 16:24-25

We tend to hold onto our perceptions of how the world should be, and we want to get ourselves and everyone else in line with our way. But Jesus says: "Follow me" (v24).

Describe the difficulty in letting go of "your way" and following Jesus' example and teachings in areas of your life you are adamant about even when you discover they go against biblical principles.

What does Jesus say we will gain if we trade our agenda for His?

Application

As humans created in God's image, striving for perfection is generally driven by a desire to do what is morally right. As we have discussed, problems develop when we expect ourselves and others to accomplish perfection relying on human effort alone. Eugene Peterson in *The Message* paraphrase translation of the Bible puts it this way:

"And now what the law code asked for but we couldn't deliver is accomplished as we, instead of redoubling our own efforts, simply embrace what the Spirit is doing in us. Those who think they can do it on their own end up obsessed with measuring their own moral muscle but never get around to exercising it in real life. Those who trust God's action in them find that God's Spirit is in them—living and breathing God!" (Romans 8:4-5)

There is a difference between expecting perfection from ourselves and others and expecting God to work His perfection through us.

Are you seeking perfection from yourself and others or allowing God's perfection to work in you?

One way to develop godly perfection is by utilizing the power of prayer. If we prayed about every person and situation that frustrated us, we would be a lot less frustrated. Prayer is an antidote for the resentment that builds up when people and circumstances do not measure up to our standard of perfection (see Philippians 4:6-8).

What things or people (without naming them) have you been trying to control or change that you will turn over to God?

Write a prayer on what you would like God to do in your life based on what you have learned from this session.

Session 2

The Image of God in You—Relating to Performance

Personal Preparation: Getting Ready for Session Two

And how do you benefit if you gain the whole world but lose your own soul in the process? Is anything worth more than your soul (Matthew 16:26)?

Meet with God

Personal Notes

Take 30 minutes each day to be alone with God in meditation and prayer. Read Romans 4.

May the Holy Spirit guide you during this session.

Describe the most positive thing you can remember from your childhood.

Self-Awareness

Character Trait	Seems Natural, Makes Life Hard	Seems Hard, Makes Life Good
Performance	I strive to accomplish many things each day in order to feel a sense of value and worth.	I can find comfort and rest in knowing that who I am is more important than what I can do. I accept that despite my weaknesses and failures, I am loved.

Group Member's Guide: *Where Is the Image of God in You?*, Living Free, P. O. Box 22127, Chattanooga, TN 37422-2127 Session 2 11

Desiring to perform at a level of excellence is admirable. The problem is we are not created to be excellent at everything. The world seems to expect us to be, however, and we sometimes take on unrealistic views of what to expect from ourselves. "We with perseverance can be mature and complete, not lacking anything" (James 1:4).

The possibility of trying to earn God's and others' love through how we perform, what we do, and what we accomplish can tend to overshadow being loved for who we are. You may have heard it said that we are human beings, not human "doings."

Describe what you perceive to be the difference between viewing your worth based on what you do versus who you are.

A key to focusing on our worth from the standpoint of who we are is to focus on who God is and what He has done. Our performance will always fall short until we realize that it is by our faith in Him, not by what we do, that we get credited with a worthy "performance."

Jesus marveled at the faith of some He healed. (i.e., Matthew 8:10, 9:22, 15:28; Mark 10:52; Luke 7:50, 17:19, 18:42). What is so fascinating about this is that the very faith Jesus marveled at came from Him according to the Bible (see Hebrews 12:2).

Describe how performing to earn God's and others' love, acceptance, and approval by our accomplishments [performance] is a demonstration of our lack of faith in God through Jesus Christ (see Romans 4:1-3).

Spiritual-Awareness

God performs in a holy way. "Who else among the gods is like you O LORD? Who is glorious in holiness like you—so awesome in splendor, performing such wonders" (Exodus 15:11)?

Ephesians 2:10

This verse talks about doing things, but first it states something about who we are.

Who does this verse say we are?

What is the purpose for which He created us?

A key phrase in this verse says there are "good things he planned for us." These are not things *we* plan in order to please others or do to be accepted by God. If we are God's masterpiece, we can *perform* out of who we are instead of primarily focusing on what we can do. We can function out of being made "anew in Christ Jesus."

John 15:5

This verse expands the thought process from Ephesians 2:10. Our performance is successful—we "produce much fruit"—because we have faith in our connection to God through Jesus Christ.

How does this verse describe our connection to God?

We are plenty busy yet often bored. Maybe it is because we are striving in our own strength and with our own agenda, leaving Jesus out of the equation.

What does this verse say we can do on our own without Jesus?

What does it mean that without Him [Jesus], we can do nothing?

If you have not turned your life over to the lordship of Jesus Christ, now would be a good time. See page 82 in this workbook for guidelines.

Philippians 3:3

Striving at performance displays confidence in what we can do.

What does this verse say about *where not* and *where to* place our confidence?

2 Corinthians 12:5-6, 9

People focused on their own performance and comparing themselves with others are reluctant to accept any kind of failure or admit any weakness. However, God's ways are often counterintuitive to human thinking.

What do these verses say about human weaknesses?

Can any good come out of weaknesses and failures in your life?

Matthew 16:24-26

What type of *performance* does verse 24 require of us to be considered a follower of Jesus?

In verse 25, what do we have to lose and to gain?

What does verse 26 say is more important to keep [save] than gaining the whole world?

Performance, what we accomplish, is eternally important when we allow it to flow out of who we are in Christ. How we perform in worldly terms can be measured. What God has done for us through Jesus Christ and what we accomplish as His children are immeasurable.

These verses describe the difference between a worldly and a godly agenda. If we are only focused on accomplishing things for personal gain, we are not accomplishing the Lord's agenda.

Application

Neil Anderson says in his book, *Victory Over the Darkness*:
> Is who you are determined by what you do, or is what you do determined by who you are? That is an important question, especially as it relates to Christian maturity. I subscribe to the latter. I believe that your hope for growth, meaning and fulfillment as a Christian is based on understanding who you are—specifically, your identity in Christ as a child of God. Your understanding of who God is and who you are in relationship to Him is the critical foundation for your belief system and your behavior patterns as a Christian (24).

Romans 4:10 expresses this principle.

The world seems to go faster all the time, and we seem to be busier all the time. If we look at the example of Jesus, however, we see swarms of people around Him, plenty to keep Him busy; and He was always in high demand. Yet He took time alone to pray (be) to His Father in heaven, to visit with friends and new acquaintances, and to rest when He had the chance—even in the midst of a storm (Matthew 8:24). Jesus never appeared to be frantic.

Can it be that we can still follow Jesus' example today? Can we actually slow down as the world speeds up? Might our performance improve and might we be more productive if we quit striving so hard?

List some things you can do to reduce the stress in your life, to take a break and rest each week, to spend more time being with God—soaking in His presence.

Write a prayer on what you would like God to do in your life based on what you have learned from this session.

Session 3: The Image of God in You—Relating to Pleasure

Personal Preparation: Getting Ready for Session Three

For you created everything, and it is for your pleasure that they exist and were created (Revelation 4:11b).

Meet with God

Personal Notes

Take 30 minutes each day to be alone with God in meditation and prayer. Read Ecclesiastes 3, 5, 8, 11, and 12.

May God grant you wisdom during this session.

Describe the most fun time you can remember. (If lots of memories come to mind, pleasure is probably a big deal to you!)

Self-Awareness

Character Trait	Seems Natural, Makes Life Hard	Seems Hard, Makes Life Good
Pleasure	Give me more, more, more. "Eat, drink, and be merry, for tomorrow we may die." In pursuing mostly fun activities, I try to avoid trudging through the harder parts of life.	I am willing to accept the bad with the good. I appreciate balance and moderation. I enjoy seasons of pleasure, not pleasure as all there is to this life.

Group Member's Guide: *Where Is the Image of God in You?*, Living Free, P. O. Box 22127, Chattanooga, TN 37422-2127

How important is it to you to incorporate fun as an ingredient in your day or week?

How big a role does pleasure play in your life?

Rymer loves to do pre-marriage counseling. Part of the process is exploring how engaged couples spend time and money alone, together, and with others. He often encounters individuals who consider fun and pleasure to be such an important part of their lives that he recommends they include "fun" as a separate category in their household budgets. That rather takes all the fun out of it—now the couple is charged with putting limits on their fun.

Is fun all there is to life? Is life about pleasure above all else? Or do we need limits on how we deal with the pursuit of pleasure?

What is your opinion?

Pleasure can be serious business. In Nehemiah 8, an assembly of Israelites was instructed to enjoy themselves. They had just listened to a reading of the sacred Scriptures and were crying and mourning over how poorly they had been paying attention to God's Word regarding how to live purposefully and reverently. It is interesting to see how preceding and following a time of pleasure were periods of studying the "Book of the Law" (See Nehemiah 8:1-2, 13).

After hearing the reading of Scripture, the Israelites were told to "Go and celebrate with a feast of choice foods and sweet drinks, and share gifts of food with people who have nothing prepared. This is a sacred day before our Lord. Don't be dejected and sad, for the joy of the Lord is your strength!" (Nehemiah 8:10)

So in order to pursue pleasure sensibly, we need to include God—be grounded in God's life instructions according to Scripture.

How do you relate to the concept of including God in your pursuits of pleasure? What happens when you leave God out?

Spiritual-Awareness

Holiness and pleasure can coexist. "For the kingdom of God is not a matter of what we eat or drink, but of living a life of goodness and peace and joy in the Holy Spirit" (Romans 14:17).

1 Corinthians 6:12-13

Part of the culture we are exposed to says: "Do your own thing. Do whatever you want as long as it doesn't hurt anybody else. Whatever you think is right is right for you; who am I to judge? You should try everything at least once."

Though verse 13 speaks specifically to sexual immorality, the principle in these verses can apply to anything.

What do these verses say about pursuing anything that seems pleasurable to us?

Ecclesiastes 8:6-8

It would be nice if this life were all pleasurable, but it is not. We cannot ultimately avoid or escape hardships.

What does verse 8 say will not rescue us?

Proverbs 21:17

"You're addicted to thrills? What an empty life! The pursuit of pleasure is never satisfied"(THE MESSAGE).

Why do you think pursuing pleasure for pleasure's sake is not satisfying?

Luke 9:24-25

What do these verses tell us happens when we consider only ourselves in our life pursuits without considering Jesus in the equation?

Paul writes, "You should also know this, Timothy, that in the last days there will be very difficult times . . . . [people will] love pleasure rather than God" (2 Timothy 3:1,4b).

John 10:9-10

Now for the Good News! When we follow God's way—pursue life including pleasure according to His Son, Jesus—what do we gain?

Revelation 4:11

God created everything. What purpose for creation does John give in this verse?

Psalm 16:11

What benefit does David describe concerning living with God forever?

Application

How do we improve the ways we view and pursue pleasure? One answer is in *The Message* version of Proverbs 16:32-33.

> Moderation is better than muscle,
> self-control better than political power.
> Make your motions and cast your votes,
> but GOD has the final say.

We improve the ways we view and pursue pleasure through practicing moderation and self-control.

Describe how you can, with God's help, exert more moderation and self-control around your views and pursuits of pleasure.

Write a prayer on what you would like God to do in your life based on what you have learned from this session.

Session 4: The Image of God in You—Relating to Determination

Personal Preparation: Getting Ready for Session Four

For my determination is to gather the nations, that I might assemble the Kingdom (Zephaniah 3:8b KJV).

Meet with God

Personal Notes

Take 30 minutes each day to be alone with God in meditation and prayer. Read Exodus 2-3 and Romans 12:9-21.

May God strengthen our character as the Holy Spirit reveals the path of Christlikeness.

Describe how you handle crisis situations or difficult tasks or people when you are under pressure. Is that when you are at your best or your worst?

Self-Awareness

Character Trait	Seems Natural, Makes Life Hard	Seems Hard, Makes Life Good
Determination	When I don't agree with, like, or think it is fair the way things are being done, I feel compelled to take charge immediately.	I will choose my battles wisely. While being bold to stand against what I believe to be wrong and stand for what I think is right, I will control my anger and consider God and others in my approach.

22 Session 4   Group Member's Guide: *Where Is the Image of God in You?*, Living Free, P. O. Box 22127, Chattanooga, TN 37422-2127

A lot of folks Rymer sees in marriage counseling have a high degree of determination. That does not mean it is impossible for them to change their minds or their ways. It just means it probably will not happen without a fight. It is not uncommon for a spouse to say after a grueling counseling session where they appeared to be upset with everything that occurred: "That was a hard session, but it sure was good!" Determined people are often willing to do whatever it takes to accomplish something that is important to them. They are generally not afraid of a fight. The question becomes: Will they fight fair?

Ken Sande, the founder of Peacemaker® Ministries, says there are three primary approaches to conflict. Peace-Fakers: those "more interested in avoiding conflict than in resolving it"—*peace at all costs*; Peace-Breakers: those "more interested in winning conflict than in preserving a relationship"; and Peace-Makers: those who look for "mutually agreeable solutions to conflict"—win-win solutions (22-25).

Describe your approach to conflict related to these three descriptions.

Why are we talking about conflict as a central discussion to the character trait of determination? It seems the things we are determined about generally involve some level of confrontation, so it is important for us to reflect on how we handle conflict as a benchmark for developing a healthy and godly use of determination as a part of our character.

How would you describe your emotions, tone of voice, body language, etc., when you are trying to get your point across regarding something you are absolutely determined about?

Let's use Moses as an example of someone with a lot of determination. In Exodus 2, we see that Moses was determined not to allow an Egyptian to mistreat a Hebrew slave.

What did Moses do when he witnessed this? (verse 12)

Rymer shares: "When my son was twelve years old and I was yelling at him for something he said that I didn't like, he said, 'I believe you have an anger problem.' Indeed I did."

So it was with Moses. When he took things into his own hands, apart from God, it was obvious he had an anger problem. From the way he handled this incident, Moses lost credibility with his own people and was rendered ineffective in helping them for many years as the Egyptian pharaoh issued an order for Moses to be arrested and killed. He had to flee the country (vv14-15).

Have you ever handled something out of misguided anger that caused more of a problem than a solution? Describe.

Spiritual-Awareness

Moses knew what it was to be changed by a holy God. "And then take on an entirely new way of life—a God-fashioned life, a life renewed from the inside and working itself into your conduct as God accurately reproduces his character in you" (Ephesians 4:22b-24, THE MESSAGE).

Exodus 3:9-12

Years after Moses fled for his life, he had an encounter with God. God chose Moses to lead the Israelites out of Egyptian oppression. With God's hand on him, Moses would later show a godly determination because "he had his eye on the One no eye could see, and kept right on going" (Hebrews 11:27b, THE MESSAGE).

What was different this time from the Exodus 2:12 incident where Moses killed the Egyptian?

Exodus 6:1-7

Though God chose Moses to lead His people, who was really accomplishing the desired results according to these verses?

Exodus 33:12-14

This is a very different Moses than the younger, less mature Moses we saw earlier who took situations into his own hands. Now Moses, still full of determination to see the best for the Israelites, does not want to do anything without God with him.

What are the indications of this in these verses?

Numbers 20:6-12

In this passage Moses permits his determination to override God's command.

How did he disobey?

What did this disobedience cost him?

Despite his mistakes, Moses did not give up nor did God give up on him. He was a great leader.

Numbers 12:3

What quality does verse 3 indicate is helpful to go along with determination in order to handle things in a godly way?

Application

When you feel determined to get your way or when you have determination to see justice done in a situation, what are steps you can take to help bring about constructive solutions rather than destructive words or actions?

From the example of Moses, we can see the value of being in close relationship with God in order to make a difference in how we handle our determination in the circumstances of life. Remember how Moses initially took things into his own hands and tried to control people. As he grew in a relationship with God, he relied more on God to control people and circumstances and became very humble. This does not mean he was any less bold. His boldness was just rooted in God, not in himself (see Ephesians 4:31).

Moses was commended by God "There has never been another prophet like Moses, whom the LORD knew face to face" (Deuteronomy 34:10).

If you are currently feeling determined about a relationship or other situation, consider how to proceed based on the resources God gives us.

The Spirit of God
What do you think the Lord wants you to do based on your prayers about the situation?

The Word of God
Have you looked in the Bible for principles that would apply to your situation?

If so, what have you discovered?

If not, where would you look?

The People of God
Have you consulted mature Christian friends? If so, how has that been helpful? If not, who would you consult?

We briefly mentioned anger earlier in this session. How do you think relying less on yourself and more on God to handle your anger in situations you have determination about is helpful?

Write a prayer on what you would like God to do in your life based on what you have learned from this session.

Session  *The Image of God in You—Relating to Servanthood*

Personal Preparation: Getting Ready for Session Five

For even I, the Son of Man, came here not to be served but to serve others, and to give my life as a ransom for many (Mark 10:45).

Meet with God

Personal Notes

Take 30 minutes each day to be alone with God in meditation and prayer. Read Mark 10:35-45.

May the Holy Spirit provide insight in this session as to the uniqueness of each group member.

What is your favorite thing to do during leisure time?

Self-Awareness

Character Trait	Seems Natural, Makes Life Hard	Seems Hard, Makes Life Good
Servanthood	I am compelled to be helpful to others in a way that makes me feel good. I often prefer to please someone rather than consider if what they want is reasonable or wise.	I will move in and out of others' lives according to what is best, wise, and healthy, not solely on what I or they desire.

Following are things often heard in counseling sessions. Have you ever experienced any of these thoughts or feelings?

- "If I don't help this person, no one will."
- "I am the only one who knows how to please this person."
- "This is the last time I am going to help this person."
- "I am tired of being a doormat."
- "I am going to stay around this person because I believe they will change."
- "If I continue to do my best to help, I believe things will get better."
- "I have to help this person because their poor choices are my fault."
- "I am a bad person if I don't do what this person wants of me."

Servanthood is meant to be something we do voluntarily. Sometimes, however, we may feel we should do something for others for reasons we feel pressured into from outside sources of intimidation or inner sources of guilt. We may not realize we are doing some things for reasons other than a sincere and healthy desire to do them. Servanthood seems worthwhile when we can serve others freely, with healthy boundaries, and with no strings attached.

We may not be aware that wrong motives for serving others can come from an unhealthy view of ourselves. We may become enmeshed with a spouse, family member, or friend in a way that we think they will not survive without us. We try to be their savior. We may not be aware that we are serving others to make ourselves feel better about ourselves. This can develop into a cycle of codependency and enabling. A major aspect of codependency is the desire to change another person in a way that only God can. We come to believe that we will eventually succeed in changing a friend or loved one's behaviors and choices that keep getting them into undesirable circumstances. Enabling is basically rescuing people repeatedly instead of allowing them to experience the consequences of their behavior which might encourage them to change. Both of these patterns can become addictive in the sense that they are hard to stop. Feelings of guilt can develop from within, and a sense of intimidation may develop from a person we have become codependent with or are enabling.

Without mentioning names, describe a time when you did something for someone because you felt intimidated. Do you know how you got into this situation?

Describe something or some things you do for others out of guilt. Do you know the source of this guilt?

True servanthood takes more than just compassion or even desire, fortitude or ability. Servanthood in the life of a maturing Christian follows a pattern from self- or worldly-centered service to God-centered service. Jesus had compassion (Mark 6:34) but stuck to His Father's plan with regards to how He served (John 5:30). We may have instinctive desires to serve others, but we may have difficulty saying "no" at appropriate times or confuse our worth to others based on what we do for them. Eugene Peterson in *The Message* paraphrase version of Philippians 1:9-11 puts it this way:

> So this is my prayer: that your love will flourish and that you will not only love much but well. Learn to love appropriately. You need to use your head and test your feelings so that your love is sincere and intelligent, not sentimental gush. Live a lover's life, circumspect and exemplary, a life Jesus will be proud of: bountiful in fruits from the soul, making Jesus Christ attractive to all, getting everyone involved in the glory and praise of God.

We can see from these verses that we "learn" to love in a way that glorifies God. The purpose of loving (and serving) others comes out of a desire to make Jesus Christ "attractive to all" as it says in the last sentence of these verses. We grow into a healthy form of servanthood when we serve out of a "sincere and intelligent" love that is focused on God.

Describe the difference in servanthood based on gaining something for yourself (or trying to be God in someone else's life) and servanthood based on bringing about God's purposes in someone else's life in a way that results in glory and praise to God.

Spiritual-Awareness

We see the holiness of Christ Jesus in His attitude toward servanthood. "Who, being in very nature God, did not consider equality with God something to be grasped, but made himself nothing, taking the very nature of a servant, being made in human likeness" (Philippians 2:6-7 NIV).

Matthew 5:37

Some with a heart of servanthood find it hard to say *no* when asked or compelled to do things for others. We are not God. We cannot be all things to anyone, much less all people.

It is good to "promise what you can deliver and deliver what you promise." This verse can apply to that concept.

Describe a time you said *yes* and found it hard to keep your commitment because you were taking on more than you could handle.

When do you find it hard to say *no*?

Psalm 15:4

What does this verse say to do when we commit to do something?

Therefore, it is wise to choose our commitments carefully and for the right reasons.

John 3:16-17

We often do things for God and others in order to be loved or make ourselves feel worthy of love.

What do these verses say we need to do in order for God to love us?

We begin to see from these verses that it takes faith to accept that we are loved by God without having to do anything.

Mark 10:42-45

These verses describe how followers of Jesus are to be different—even in leadership roles.

According to verse 43, what does Jesus say the qualification for being a leader is?

In verse 45 how does Jesus demonstrate His leadership?

Servanthood comes from an attitude of worship and thankfulness for who God is, what He has done, and what He is going to do. One of the ways you can overcome struggles in your life is to "count your blessings." Write down things you are thankful for, especially when you are going through trials.

List ways you can become free from intimidation.

List ways you can quit doing things out of guilt.

List ways you can say *no* in order to establish healthy boundaries so that you can maintain proper rest and focus in your life.

Write a prayer on what you would like God to do in your life based on what you have learned from this session.

Session 6: The Image of God in You—Relating to Passion

Personal Preparation: Getting Ready for Session Six

To whom also he showed himself alive after his passion by many infallible proofs (Acts 1:3 KJV).

Meet with God

Personal Notes

Take 30 minutes each day to be alone with God in meditation and prayer. Read Philippians 1.

May you experience God's faithful presence in this session.

Describe something you are passionate about.

Self-Awareness

Character Trait	Seems Natural, Makes Life Hard	Seems Hard, Makes Life Good
Passion	I allow my emotions to rule my actions and perspectives of my relationships and circumstances.	I love the beauty in the world and appreciate the richness of the relationships and blessings I have.

Rymer usually asks a couple at the start of a marriage counseling session how things are going. Some people tell him they judge how their life is going based on whatever emotional state they are experiencing at that moment.

Passion (the object of strong desire) is something many have. We will discuss passion as something closely related to emotions. As illustrated in the example above, it appears some people experience and express life through emotion more than others. However, we all have emotions and passions, so we can all relate to the concepts in this session to some degree.

34 Session 6   Group Member's Guide: *Where Is the Image of God in You?*, Living Free, P. O. Box 22127, Chattanooga, TN 37422-2127

We can have passion that is full of hope and joyful expectancy, or we can have passion that is fearfully angry or sad.

We can have passion that moves us towards relationships or goals in life, or we can push away when we find it hard to believe someone might actually receive us just as we are. We find it hard to believe reaching a goal is possible or will be lasting. This type of passion or longing tells us: "This is too good to be true," or "This won't last."

There is a form of passion that is never quite satisfied with the way things are because it longs for something or someone we once had that is now missing in our life.

Passion can propel us into healthy relationships, or it can push us into isolation.

You may have experienced some of these positive and negative aspects of passion.

Describe how you relate or do not relate to one or more of these concepts.

There is a form of passion that is hopeful and a form that is hopeless. Hopeful passion may reflect on the past or be hopeful about the future, but it is content in the *now*. Hopeless passion doubts—doubts that things can ever be as good as they seemed in the past or be as good as hoped for in the future. In a sense, hopeless passion believes more in the past than in the present or future so it conjures up hopelessness *now* based primarily on feelings, not necessarily on truth.

Some people who live out of a great sense of passion are the artists among us. Some of them live out joyful, exuberant expressions of life while others live in a melancholy world full of disappointments and disillusions.

What do you think makes the difference?

Hopeful passion excites and motivates us to imagine and be a part of life that is vibrant no matter our circumstances or emotions. Jesus talked about that kind of life in John 10:10. Here we could say that hopeless passion is motivated by "the thief" and hopeful passion is God-motivated and God-centered.

Passion can include suffering. However, it is suffering with a purpose. In Philippians 1:29, Paul even says that suffering for Christ is a privilege.

Hopeful passion motivates us to realize our purpose and keep us focused on a mission. Again, no matter the circumstances or how Jesus felt, His passion for the mission of the cross was never deterred or extinguished and the Apostle Paul's passion to share Christ was seemingly inexhaustible.

Jesus had passion, but it never deterred him from the mission for which His Father sent Him, and He lived life with all His being focused on the same passion His heavenly Father had (John 5:19).

There is a difference between having passion for something and being completely absorbed by something or someone other than God.

What is the difference?

Spiritual-Awareness

With Gethsemane and Calvary ahead of Him, Jesus said to His father, "For them I sanctify myself, that they too may be truly sanctified" (John 17:19 NIV). Andrew Murray states, "Holiness is the full entrance of our will into God's will" (p152). Jesus had a holy passion for the cross to free us from the power of sin.

Romans 12:6-8

These verses indicate how God *wires* each of us uniquely to have passion in different ways.

How do the *gifts* He gives us motivate our passion?

Romans 12:9-11

These verses draw us back to the theme of our study into how we are individually and corporately made in the image of God. The primary focus is not on passion, other traits, or the gifts discussed in Romans 12:6-8 but on love.

These verses instruct us on how to use the unique gifts, traits, and talents God has given us in a lovingly passionate way.

What are some of the words and phrases we can be passionate about in these verses?

Romans 12:12

In our passion and zeal for life, we can get off track when things do not go the way we expect them to or when people fail us in ways that are hurtful or upsetting. This verse acknowledges the trouble we may encounter.

What does it tell us to do?

1 Kings 19:4, 10; Jonah 4:3; Jeremiah 20:18

People of great passion can fall prey to stress, anger, depression, and despair or just a plain "I don't care" attitude—especially when they are focused on what is wrong in life rather than on what is right and what God is doing to make things right. Passionate people can find themselves in very dark places at times.

What are some of the emotions you see in these verses?

1 Kings 19:6-8; Jonah 4:6, 10-11; Jeremiah 20:11-13, 29:11-14

These verses indicate how these men were encouraged by God to pull out of the hopeless emotional state they were experiencing.
What are some of the things they and the Lord did?

What are some of the things they and the Lord did?

Psalm 139:21-24

As mentioned earlier, many people of strong passion are expressive in the arts. David, who wrote this "song," was a musician, among other things (shepherd, warrior, king). In the earlier verse we studied, Romans 12:9, we are instructed to "hate what is wrong" or evil. It does not say to hate people; the verse is all about love. In our humanness it is hard to separate the two. David sensed he was passionate in an ungodly way.

What did he conclude in verse 24 he needed in order to turn his ungodly passion into godly passion?

Application

As stated previously in this session, many people of great passion are artists—writers, painters, musicians, actors, dancers, journalists, performers, etc. Art in its many forms is powerful and influences us in many ways. Art expresses passion, drama, and emotion.

Art is also very subjective. What appeals to one person may not appeal to another. What seems negative or positive to one person may not seem negative or positive to you.

The art we participate in and expose ourselves to tells a lot about the focus of our passion.

1 Corinthians 10:31 says: "Whatever you eat or drink or whatever you do, you must do all for the glory of God."

Are the art forms you expose yourself to positive for you? Is your participation or observance of the art forms you are exposed to glorifying to God?

In becoming more aware of the art forms you are exposed to, what changes do you think you need to make with regards to the type of art you "eat or drink" (consume)?

When we give up something, we generally need to fill that void with something else.

If you reduce or eliminate some of the types of movies you watch, books or magazines you read, news, internet, radio, music, plays, and the like, what will you fill the void with?

Might you simply need more "stillness" in your life? Psalm 46:10: "Be silent, and know I am God!"

How can you build times of silence or stillness into your life?

When and how will you fit this into your schedule?

As we mentioned earlier, hopeful passion is God and others centered. We are passionate about things that glorify God and help others in some way. The Apostle Paul remained God-focused in his passion for the Lord despite many difficulties and said: "For I have learned to be content whatever the circumstances" (Philippians 4:11 NIV).

List one thing you will do this week to ground yourself in things that more clearly reflect or represent God's passions.

How will what you have learned and what you plan to change help you be content no matter what is happening?

Be encouraged. You are not in this work alone: "Being confident of this, that he [God] who began a good work in you will carry it on to completion until the day of Christ Jesus" (Philippians 1:6 NIV). I have heard the sum of all the commandments as Jesus expressed in Matthew 22:37-40 paraphrased in the following way: "Love God, love others [love life]!"

Now that is real passion!

Write a prayer on what you would like God to do in your life based on what you have learned from this session.

Session 7: The Image of God in You—Relating to Inquiry — consultar

Personal Preparation: Getting Ready for Session Seven

The LORD God called to Adam, "Where are you?" (Genesis 3:9).

Meet with God

Personal Notes

Take 30 minutes each day to be alone with God in meditation and prayer. Read 1 John 4-5.

May you experience the love of God in this session.

Describe something you are certain about and something you wish you were more certain of. (If you feel you are certain of almost nothing and uncertain about most everything, this session may be especially for you!)

Self-Awareness

Character Trait	Seems Natural, Makes Life Hard	Seems Hard, Makes Life Good
Inquiry	I am fearful and doubtful of many things in life. I sense there is much to question in order to find assurance.	Because of my faith in God, I can grow in trust and confidence that I am secure in His plan for my life.

People ask questions and inquire about things for different reasons. In this session we will focus on inquiry as a process some people use to overcome doubt and dispel fear. This could be fear of threats to health, relationships, provision, happiness— almost anything you can think of.

Before we talk about inquiry related to doubt and fear, however, let us look at some aspects of inquiry in general.

Inquiry is about asking questions and seeking answers. Let us explore the nature of our questions surrounding our search for satisfying answers. Are we asking the right questions? Are we asking enough questions? Are we asking too many questions? Are we asking the right people? Are we seeking answers in the right places? Do we need an answer to all of our questions? Are there some things we are better off not knowing? Is it okay to inquire about whatever comes to mind?

What do you think about one or more of these questions?

Let us look at inquiry related to doubt and fear. Doubt and fear are sometimes viewed as the same. For purposes of our discussion, however, let us look at them separately. Consider doubt a roadblock to something you want to believe, something you feel you know in your head but are having a hard time convincing your heart. It could be something that is true or something you think or want to be true.

Can you think of something that falls into this category for you?

What about fear? Let us consider fear the expectation of or anticipation of some evil or danger we feel certain we are going to experience. We feel certain something bad is going to happen to us.

What do you fear most in life, and what types of questions would you like answers for to dispel this fear?

Doubting something good about God, others, ourselves, or our circumstances can lead to fear that something bad is going to happen to us rather than focusing on the good things that are happening or might happen in the future.

Granted, some doubts and fears are legitimate and true. We will concentrate our discussions around doubts and fears that dwell on negative rather than positive views of life—doubts and fears that are contrary to God's love and the promises He conveys to us through the Bible and in other ways.

Questions alone do not give us relief from doubt and fear. Answers do. Just as it is important to ask the right questions, it is important to search in the right places for the best answers, answers we can trust.

In the Bible we find that faith overcomes doubt and love dispels fear. 1 John 4:16-18 tells us the ultimate answer to fear is love. Knowing the true nature of God's love puts in us a trust or faith that casts our fears away.

What do these verses say about God?

These verses also indicate that our ultimate fear is judgment—in some versions it is translated as "punishment," referring specifically to God's judgment. But could this principle apply to other relationships? Do we utilize inquiry to dispel fears of threats to health, relationships, or provision because we fear we are being judged or punished by God, authorities over us, family members, bosses, teachers, coaches, pastors, friends, family members, and others? Do we feel we deserve this punishment? Is this just a temporary punishment? Are we under eternal judgment? Is there a way out? Do we know the way out? More questions. Let's look for answers to these questions in the Spiritual-Awareness portion of this session.

Spiritual-Awareness

Am I the only person in this predicament—having reason to fear judgment?

Romans 3:23

What is the answer to the above question based on this verse?

Is there a way out of this predicament and this fear? Is there a way out for me?

Romans 3:22, 24-26

These verses which surround the previous verse have good news. What is it?

Romans 10:8-11

Here is more good news. Many times it helps to voice our doubts and questions out loud. In the same way, it helps to speak answers and truths out loud.

What does verse 9 say about the importance of our words?

We sometimes say: "I know the truth in my head, but I cannot get it into my heart." Speaking the truth out loud is one way to get something from a thought in our head into our heart as a belief according to this verse.

Verse 11 tells us that "anyone who believes in him will not be disappointed." We may still have some questions, but how do these words give you comfort?

What if I need more convincing than the average person?

John 20:24-29

Jesus is willing to go to great lengths to help us believe He is God and trustworthy to be our Savior and Lord. Thomas had grave doubts about this.

What evidence did Thomas think he needed to believe Jesus was the resurrected Lord?

Interestingly, Thomas thought he needed to touch Jesus in order to believe, but he only needed to see. Clearly, some of us need more convincing than others, but sometimes we need less convincing than we think. (Notice in verse 28 Thomas spoke with his mouth and thus believed in his heart as we mentioned in the previous verses in Romans 10:8-11.)

In verse 29 Jesus talks about people who must see in order to believe.

What does Jesus say about faith that believes without seeing?

Okay, what if I still feel like I'm under judgment?

Romans 8:1, 31-37

These verses say much about how God judges us as well as His views on our judgments as well as others' judgments of us.

What does verse 1 say about judgment of those who belong to Christ?

Verses 31-37 say we will have troubles but gives us several assurances that proclaim ultimate victory.

What are some of these assurances?

Psalm 27:1

The Psalms offer many words of comfort regarding God's protection.

What does this verse say about our fears of danger?

Romans 10:17

How does this verse say we get faith?

It is interesting that this verse talks about listening or hearing. This implies that our faith journey is not something we do alone or in isolation.

What about security and loyalty?

Psalm 112:7-8

What do these verses tell us about security?

A secure relationship with God helps us in our relationships with others.

Psalm 27:10

What does this verse say about loyalty?

We desire security and loyalty in our human relationships. However, perfect security and loyalty can only come from God. As we grow in His love, our fears and doubts can be overcome and this can bring comfort and wisdom to all our relationships.

Application

God asks questions for our benefit. He already knows the answers because He is omniscient (all knowing). "Make them pure and holy by teaching them your words of truth" (John 17:17).

How can I overcome doubt and fear?

Hebrews 11:1 tells us that faith "is the confident assurance that what we hope for is going to happen. It is the evidence of things we cannot yet see."

1 John 4:18 tells us that God's love growing, maturing, and becoming perfected in us "has no fear, because perfect love expels all fear."

Faith is an antidote for doubt and love is an antidote for fear regarding "things we cannot yet see" or do not see clearly (see 1 Corinthians 13:12 on the next page).

What do I do to develop my faith and love?

This involves spiritual and emotional growth, and it is a process.

The Apostle Paul says in 1 Corinthians 13:11-13:

> It's like this: When I was a child, I spoke and thought and reasoned as a child does. But when I grew up, I put away childish things. Now we see things imperfectly as in a poor mirror, but then we will see everything with perfect clarity. All that I know now is partial and incomplete, but then I will know everything completely, just as God knows me now. There are three things that will endure—faith, hope and love—and the greatest of these is love.

1 John 4:17 says: "As we live in God, our love grows more perfect. So we will not be afraid on the day of judgment, but we can face him with confidence because we are like Christ here in this world."

So this becomes a process of replacing worry about things that could go wrong with hope that things will go right. As Rymer's wife says: "It's an openness to trust."

Let us explore two questions from 1 John 4:17 as we come to a close of this session regarding inquiry.

How can we best live in God so our love will grow more perfect? List at least five things.

What will you do to "become more like Christ in this world?" List at least three things, one of which you will start this week.

How will this help you with the question you answered earlier in this session about what you fear the most?

As we grow more like Christ and as we follow Him and grow in our relationship with God through Jesus, we find places in our lives where we no longer feel a need to have all our questions answered. We feel secure in His love.

Write a prayer on what you would like God to do in your life based on what you have learned from this session.

Session 8: The Image of God in You—Relating to Examination

Personal Preparation: Getting Ready for Session Eight

Test me O LORD, and try me, examine my heart and my mind (Psalm 26:2 NIV).

Meet with God

Personal Notes

Take 30 minutes each day to be alone with God in meditation and prayer. Read Proverbs 3.

May God grant you wisdom and understanding to comprehend what He is revealing in this session.

Describe how you analyze things. Do you tend to "work things out in your head" before you speak, or do you tend to "think out loud" as you go?

Self-Awareness

Character Trait	Seems Natural, Makes Life Hard	Seems Hard, Makes Life Good
Examination	If I can gather enough information and be left alone long enough to examine it, I can work out any problem in life.	I will defer to God's wisdom to know when to share my thoughts and needs with others as it is through others that God often meets our needs.

There is a time for examination, analysis, and observation of life; and there is a time to engage in life, go into action. We will explore how to find a healthy balance between examination and engagement.

People with a high degree of focus on examination and analysis can have a lot of conversations going on in their heads—with themselves and others.

Rymer shares an example of this from his marriage counseling. Occasionally, a spouse will think an issue has been fully examined, discussed, and resolved while the other spouse does not feel they have had much, if any, input on the situation. Upon further investigation, what has actually occurred is one spouse has thought about the situation, considered a response, and considered their spouse's response without ever actually checking or discussing the situation with their partner. In other words, they had a conversation, but it was all in their head. The conversation seemed so real to them they did not realize that their spouse was never in on this problem-solving process!

If you can relate to that scenario, you may have a tendency to examine things mostly in your head and, it might be said, with great fervor!

If you are one who analyzes things internally and keeps fairly much to yourself or if you tend to share your feelings and opinions more openly, describe what you think are the primary reasons you are the way you are.

Let's look at examination from the standpoint of motivation.

Are we examining something or someone because it is our habit to examine? Does examination in itself make us feel secure? Is this some sort of coping mechanism?

What do you think?

Some of us try to analyze situations and relationships in a way that makes life seem simpler or less demanding. Our minds can be a place of refuge from the yearnings in our hearts. If we can explain something to our own satisfaction, we just feel better about it.

The big question becomes: What do we do when all the examination and analysis we can muster still does not resolve some of the deepest questions of our lives?

Some things we can understand and some we cannot. In the Bible, Job's friends thought they had God and life all figured out. After God allowed them to examine Job's circumstances and fully voice their opinions, God had a few questions Himself (Job 38:3).

What do you think was the purpose of God's questions?

Spiritual-Awareness

Job began his life journey with faith in God. He learned and grew through life's trials to gain a deeper faith that was "eye-opening."

On his faith journey, Job recognized God as holy, omnipotent (all powerful), and alive (Job 9:1-10). "But as for me, I know that my Redeemer lives, and that he will stand upon the earth at last. And after my body had decayed, yet in my body I will see God" (Job 19:25-26)!

Job 42:1-6

What do you think Job meant in his statement in verse 5?

Matthew 6:25-33

We sometimes examine and analyze things as a way to escape our fears or frustrations that life demands too much and there is not enough to go around—whether that be material provision, love, peace, good health, or whatever our felt needs are.

How do these verses speak to those fears or frustrations?

Verse 33 gives us something to examine and analyze. What is it?

We can examine God's Word with God's people by the power of God's Spirit to understand how to "make the Kingdom of God" our primary concern.

Proverbs 3:5-6

These verses add a dimension to wisdom and understanding that is beyond "head" knowledge.

What in verse 5 indicates understanding by other than our mind?

Proverbs 3:7-8

We can examine things in our heads all day long, but there comes a point when we need to act based on faith, our trust in the Lord (v5).

What does verse 7 say about our wisdom?

What is the result in verse 8 of our seeking his will (v6) and having a healthy fear of the Lord (v7)?

Ecclesiastes 12:11-13

The way to find balance between examination and action are found in these verses.

What do they say about this?

Application

Back to our original scenario of the spouse who worked everything out in their head without discussing things openly.

If you are like that or when you are like that, how will you trust God with all your heart and allow Him to direct your path in knowing when, if, or how you can be more open in sharing your feelings?

There is a healthy aspect to sitting back and examining situations before we speak and not speaking too much (see Proverbs 10:19 and James 1:19). There are also times when we do not want to remain silent and need to act or speak (i.e., Galatians 6:1 and James 5:16).

It is calling upon and trusting God's wisdom that we know the difference.

Write a prayer on what you would like God to do in your life based on what you have learned from this session.

Session 9: The Image of God in You—Relating to Peacefulness

Personal Preparation: Getting Ready for Session Nine

May the Lord of peace himself always give you his peace no matter what happens (2 Thessalonians 3:16a).

Meet with God

Personal Notes

Take 30 minutes each day to be alone with God in meditation and prayer. Read Philippians 4.

May God reveal himself to you through your victories and struggles.

Describe what you fear most about conflict and what you think influenced you to feel this way.

Self-Awareness

Character Trait	Seems Natural, Makes Life Hard	Seems Hard, Makes Life Good
Peacefulness	I try to be, or appear to be pleasing, agreeable, and accepting of everyone in order to maintain peace and harmony.	I will engage in relationships in a way that allows for honest, caring, and patient communication as well as trusting in God to bring about peace beyond my capabilities.

You have probably heard the expression: "They just want peace at all costs." The author of this study shares a personal testimony.

> That used to be me and still is to a certain degree. I like peacefulness. I like to be a part of family and groups that are in harmony with each other. I want to come across to people as pleasing, agreeable, and accepting of them.

For me, peacefulness became a trait I used from early childhood to try and fit in. I grew up the youngest person in my immediate family and the youngest of all my first cousins. I felt left out and unimportant in the overall scheme of things—not that that was true. It was just how I felt. I wanted to gain a greater sense of belonging. I thought always having the appearance of peacefulness would do the trick.

You may have different reasons for focusing on peacefulness, or you may not focus on it at all.

Is peacefulness a central trait for you or someone you are close to? Describe your thoughts about "peace at all costs."

The author also states:
> Notice I said earlier that I thought always having the appearance of peacefulness would give me a sense of belonging. It was not always genuine. Therefore, it wore me out just trying to keep up appearances.
>
> I became what is known as passive-aggressive. I appeared to go along willingly with what others wanted me to do, but I refused to do what I knew others wanted me to when it was not verbally stated or when they were not looking. I became angry about all the demands I felt were placed on me. I avoided people, groups, and even emotions that were not harmonious. Since that could be just about any person, group, or emotion, I tended to miss out on a lot of good things I could have experienced.

A lack of genuineness can sometimes lead us to take the blame for something that is really not our fault—just to keep the peace.

Have you ever done this? If so, describe how it worked out.

This describes the downward spiral of the negative uses of this trait. Let's explore the way to true peacefulness in the next verse.

We have a heavenly Father who accepts us for just who we are without having to put on appearances. Even in our best effort, we may not be able to be at peace with everything and everybody all the time.

Romans 12:18 says: "Do your part to live in peace with everyone, as much as possible."

What does this verse mean to you?

Spiritual-Awareness

Since God is omnipresent (present everywhere, all the time), His peace can be experienced in any place or in any circumstance. "Holy, holy, holy is the LORD Almighty! The whole earth is filled with his glory!" (Isaiah 6:3).

It has been said, "No God, no peace; know God, know peace."

Philippians 4:6-7

As we come to know God, we begin to realize that He is the source of peace, that it is through prayer with thanksgiving to God that peacefulness becomes genuine in our lives.

What do these verses have to say about how prayer with thanksgiving changes our perspective on what true peace is?

Philippians 4:8-9

Some people describe these verses as encouraging positive thinking. Actually, they are more about "truth" thinking. When we are discouraged by a lack of peacefulness, we tend to think negatively and not consider the good things that are going on. We become "worst-case scenario" thinkers.

How do these verses help to change our perspective from bad to better?

What does verse 9 say is the result of focusing in this way?

Isaiah 9:6-7

Though these verses proclaim things that have only been fulfilled in part, what hope do they give you about how Jesus Christ can rule in our hearts to bring about peacefulness now?

2 Thessalonians 3:16

When do these verses indicate we can expect peacefulness to operate in our lives?

Describe a time you did not expect God's peacefulness to be with you, but it unexplainably was or is.

Matthew 11:28-30

These verses do not speak directly to peace. However, when we are striving for peace and we become weary, our energy drained from lack of peace, how do these verses encourage us?

Matthew 5:9

What encouragement or incentive does this verse give you to seek true and lasting peacefulness?

Application

Focusing on peacefulness without putting God in the equation can lead us to disrupt the very peace we are seeking. Trying to change others and our circumstances without calling on God's help leads to frustration, negativity, and anger that can actually cause disharmony. We can stuff our frustrations until they finally explode on someone. By that point, we cannot even explain why we are angry; or we can impulsively try to shut down a conversation before God has a chance to work and the "dust can settle."

Consequently, the goal becomes what is stated in James 1:19-20: "Dear friends, be quick to listen, slow to speak, and slow to get angry. Your anger can never make things right in God's sight."

You may appear to be slow to anger, but are you really? You may appear to be slow to speak, but what are you saying inside? You may appear to be listening, but are you really hearing what may be "between the lines" of what is being said? Do you have God's peace (Philippians 4:7)? Are you as calm on the inside as you appear on the outside?

Describe ways you can improve in the areas mentioned in these verses.

How will this improve the use of the peacefulness character trait in you?

Write a prayer on what you would like God to do in your life based on what you have learned from this session.

Session 10: The Image of God in You—Relating to Your Neighbor

Personal Preparation: Getting Ready for Session Ten

Love your neighbor as yourself (Luke 10:27b).

Meet with God

Personal Notes

Take 30 minutes each day to be alone with God in meditation and prayer. Read Luke 10:25-37.

May God clearly show you the ways you are created in His image.

Describe one interesting aspect of your relationship, interaction, or lack thereof with the neighbor that lives nearest to you.

Self-Awareness

Peacefulness is the character trait to which some people strongly relate. That does not mean we are always at peace with others, ourselves, or God. Why not? As we have discussed so far in this study, we do not always use our character traits in constructive ways—ways that bring about peace. In addition to this, however, we are not always focused on the positive aspects of our own and others' character traits. The more we do that, the greater chance we have of understanding ourselves and others in a way that helps us build healthy communication patterns and relationships.

In these last three sessions, we want to draw attention to the positive ways we see each others' character traits. Hopefully this will lead us to gain a greater appreciation for the different character qualities in each of us.

Starting with this session, we will invite two or three of you to share your positive uses of the character trait you relate to the most and how you think God is working in your life to strengthen that trait.

Then we will go around the group and let each group member encourage you in how they appreciate your use of this or other positive character traits and qualities they see in you.

Some of the purposes of this exercise are as follows:

- To help you see yourself in a more positive way.
- To have the experience of receiving and accepting positive comments from others.
- To let you know that others have a positive impression of you.
- To let you know you have character qualities you may not be aware of.
- To let you know how others perceive God is working in your life.

Choose the character trait from the list of those we have studied that you relate to the most, or just pick a trait you relate to. (See the *Character Trait Chart* in the *Preface* on **page ii** as a reminder).

List some positive ways you use this trait to enhance your relationships.

In what areas of your life do you think God is working to strengthen the positive uses of this character trait?

Do we have any volunteers to start us off?

The rest of us are here as active listeners, and our goal is to *support* you in this process, not to judge or advise.

Now each of you will have an opportunity to show your loving concern for the person who shared their character trait by offering some positive feedback about what you have heard.

Each group member is given the opportunity to offer a caring, clear, and constructive view.

Was it difficult for you to receive positive comments from others?

Did you feel like denying or apologizing for a character quality mentioned?

What did you learn in this exercise?

We look forward to continuing this important process over the next two sessions. This kind of experience is valuable. It is helpful to those who have shared and to all of us as we use the principles we have learned and apply them to real-life circumstances.

In Luke 10:25-37, Jesus has a discussion regarding how God wishes us to view and treat our *neighbor*. A broad definition of neighbor would be someone who lives near us. The biblical definition as presented in the Luke 10 verses might be summed up as anyone in need of our help or kindness. In either case, this could be someone we know well, a little, or not at all. This could be someone you like quite well, a little, or not at all.

From the Luke 10:25-37 verses, would you say it makes a difference how well you know or like someone as to how you should treat them?

What do you see in these verses to support your answer?

Spiritual-Awareness

We are called to follow God and love others. "Follow God's example in everything you do, because you are his dear children. Live a life filled with love for others" (Ephesians 5:1-2).

Matthew 5:43-44

These verses not only contain deep spiritual challenges but are also very basically practical in dealing with others who have character traits we have difficulty relating to.

How do you think these verses apply to people you have a hard time communicating or dealing with?

As we love and pray for others with the love of Christ, a love beyond ourselves, we can gain a greater understanding of them as someone God loves and in whose image He desires them to be.

Leviticus 19:18

Jesus quoted this verse when he spoke of loving our neighbor as we love ourselves. When we are focused on the negative aspects of our and others' character traits, we tend to build attitudes that lead to vengeance and grudges.

How does viewing the positive aspects of others' character traits guard against this?

How does viewing ourselves negatively affect the way we view others?

It is important for us to love ourselves in the way God loves us. If we view ourselves the way God views us, we will not think more highly or lowly of ourselves than we should. (See Romans 12:3).

Hebrews 12:15

The previous verse implies a path of love to overcome revenge and grudges. In this session we have related this to focusing positively on our own and others' character qualities.

What does this verse imply overcomes building up "bitter roots" against ourselves and others?

Though this verse refers specifically to sin, viewing ourselves and others from a negative point of view without considering the positive misses the grace of God.

Romans 13:9-10

These verses continue in telling us things not to do to our neighbor.

Again, what do the verses say will keep us from treating our neighbor in an ungodly way?

Galatians 5:14-16

These verses tell us what happens when we fail to love.

What are some forms of "biting and devouring" mentioned in verse 15 that are destructive?

What is the way back to godliness towards our neighbor as mentioned in verse 16?

Application

In this session we have discussed positive ways to view different character traits. Sometimes we can even have a falsely negative view of the very nature and character of God. As a way to put what we have discovered in this session into action, please consider the following:

- In what ways have you been viewing character traits of God in a wrongly negative way and what can you do to replace these misconceptions with the truth?

- In what ways have you been negatively viewing your own character traits, and how can focusing on positive aspects of your character help you have a more balanced view of yourself?

- What can you do this week to improve your view of yourself?

- In what ways have you been focused on the negative aspects of a *neighbor's* character traits, and what can you do to improve your attitude towards this person?

- List at least one thing you will do this week to start this process.

Write a prayer on what you would like God to do in your life based on what you have learned from this session.

Session 11: The Image of God in You—Relating to Your Family

Personal Preparation: Getting Ready for Session Eleven

Anyone who does God's will is my brother and sister and mother (Mark 3:35).

Meet with God

Take 30 minutes each day to be alone with God in meditation and prayer. Read Colossians 3.

May you be uplifted in this session in a way that will bring praise and honor to God.

Describe a time with your family that was funny or memorable to you in an especially good way.

Self-Awareness

A few years ago Rymer met twice a week with a group of male inmates in our county jail for Christian discipleship and sharing. One day one of the guys said he had never experienced true love like he did in this group. Then a couple of the biggest men in the room started crying, and one guy said: "This is beautiful!" This was not a typical day with a group of guys.

What was different? One of the primary things we focused on in this group was lifting each other up, not putting each other down. We were intentionally focused on looking for the positive qualities in each other rather than focusing on the negative—the latter of which is mostly what goes on in our culture and is intensified in jail.

With that in mind, we will continue as we began in the last session to allow group members to:

- Share the character trait with which they most identify.
- Describe how they most positively use that trait.
- Describe how they think God is working in their life to strengthen that trait.

After a few minutes of sharing, we will give the other group members an opportunity to give feedback on the positive character traits and qualities they have observed and appreciate in the person who shared.

Begin the sharing. Just give feedback, not advice. And keep it

---

Sometimes our best character qualities are least appreciated or noticed in our own immediate families. Jesus dealt with this. His own brothers and sisters did not take him seriously as the Messiah until after His death and resurrection (See John 7:1-5). But God has provided us another family and another opportunity to use and display our character traits in a Christlike way. The family of God, Christ's Church, the body of Christ are all biblical ways of describing a spiritual family that transcends flesh and blood. I hope you have experienced family in this small group in a way that is functionally healthy. Neither of these families is perfected yet, but our spiritual family in Christ places us on that path. Look at the verses in Mark 3:31-35.

Who does Jesus say His brother and sister and mother are?

Desiring to do the will of God instead of being primarily focused on how we can get our own way puts us on the path to "true" family.

Spiritual-Awareness

In all of our relationships, God is calling us to be holy. "God has called us to be holy, not to live impure lives" (1 Thessalonians 4:7).

Romans 12:1-2 NIV

Here we learn more about "spiritual family" and about God's will.

What in verse 1 indicates family beyond that of flesh and blood?

What do these verses say about the will of God?

Romans 12:3-5

Here we learn not only that we are to honor each other as different and unique parts of "Christ's body" but what else also?

As stated in verse 5, in what ways do you think we need each other?

John 13:34

There are many "one another" or "each other" verses in Scripture that indicate how much we need each other in "spiritual family." This is a key verse.

Can you name others and why you think they are important?

Colossians 3:13; Matthew 6:14-15

How important is forgiveness in maintaining a right relationship with God and family?

Colossians 3:14; 1 Peter 4:8

According to these verses, what makes "spiritual family" work?

What thoughts do you have about why that is?

Application

We have focused so far this session on how to treat each other as members of God's family.

How do you think God wants you to apply these principles to your blood family?

Is there someone in your family you can be more loving towards? How will you go about doing that?

Do you have a Christian brother or sister you can be more loving to? How will you go about doing that?

Is there someone you need to forgive? What will you do about that in the next week?

Write a prayer on what you would like God to do in your life based on what you have learned from this session.

Session **12**

The Image of God in You—Relating to Your Spouse and God

Personal Preparation: Getting Ready for Session Twelve

I promised you as a pure bride to one husband, Christ (2 Corinthians 11:2b).

Meet with God

Personal Notes

Take 30 minutes each day to be alone with God in meditation and prayer. Read Isaiah 54-55 and 1 Corinthians 7.

May the Holy Spirit guide you in understanding what it means to be the Bride of Christ.

Whether you are married or not, describe what you thought about marriage when you were young and whether or not you thought marriage was for you.

Self-Awareness

This session is about your most intimate relationships—with your spouse, if you are married, and with God. We will explore how who you are in the Image of God with your unique character traits is best realized in your relationship with God and your spouse, if you have one.

Before we explore these profound mysteries, let us continue as in the previous two sessions to allow group members to:

- Share the character trait with which you most identify.
- Describe how you most positively use that trait.
- Describe how you think God is working in your life to strengthen that trait.

After a few minutes of sharing, we will give the other group members an opportunity to give feedback on the positive character traits and qualities they have observed and appreciate in the person who shared.

Begin the sharing. Just give feedback, not advice. And keep it positive!

If you are married, this session should help you understand love and intimacy on a deeper level. If you are not married, some of the biblical concepts regarding marriage should help you in your intimacy with God.

Hebrews 13:4a (NIV) says: "Marriage should be honored by all." This means all, everyone, whether or not you are married. This verse is not saying everyone needs to be married. It means marriage should be respected by those who are married, not yet married, perhaps have been married, or may never be married. In the context of this verse, The Bible is indicating that a godly marriage represents a good model for a pure and holy life, including the kind of life where you can use your character traits in the most beneficial way.

What does "Marriage should be honored by all" mean to you?

Spiritual-Awareness

God is calling us to a life free of sexual sin. "God wants you to be holy, so you should keep clear of all sexual sin. Then each of you will control your body and live in holiness and honor" (1 Thessalonians 4:3-4).

Isaiah 54:5; Ephesians 5:31-32

As marriage is the most intimate relationship we can experience humanly, these verses compare it to the type of relationship the Church (the people of God, members of the body of Christ) can experience with God.

What indicates intimacy in these verses?

What do these truths mean to you?

John 14:21

In order to know how to best use the character traits and qualities God has given us, we need to know intimately the God who created us. Let us look at indicators of love and intimacy in this verse.

What in this verse indicates to God (Jesus) that we love him?

What does this verse say is God's response to our love?

What in this verse indicates intimacy as a result of this mutual love?

1 Corinthians 6:17

What does this verse say regarding how intimate we can be with the Lord?

---

1 Corinthians 7:29-38

Whether you are married or not, what do verses 30, 32, and 34-35 indicate is most important?

What do these verses say gets in the way of what is most important?

Matthew 19:10-12

Jesus also indicates marriage may not be for everyone.

If someone decides not to marry, what does verse 12 indicate this will allow that person to be solely dedicated to?

---

1 Corinthians 7:1, 7, 17

This relates to the previous verses. We do not talk much about the gift of singleness or celibacy these days.

Though Jesus and Paul make it clear it is good to be married, when God helps (Matthew 19:11) or gifts (1 Corinthians 7:7) someone to be single, what is the advantage of this?

If you are not married, how would you try and figure out if God might be calling you to a life of celibacy and singleness?

Jesus and Paul make it clear, however, that we are to do everything we can to stay married if we are married.

Jesus said, "Since they [husband and wife] are no longer two but one, let no one separate them, for God has joined them together" (Matthew 19:6).

Application

The greater our intimacy with God, the more He can use the character traits He has given us for His purposes.

Romans 8:28-29a talk about loving God and His primary purpose for us:

> And we know that God causes everything to work together for the good of those who love God and are called according to his purpose for them. For God knew his people in advance, and he chose them to become like his Son.

Based on what you have discovered as we have gone through this study, what do you think you can add, eliminate, or change in your life that will help you become more like Jesus?

Whatever situation you find yourself in—no matter what kind of mess you may feel you have made of your life—Isaiah 54:4-8 says:

> Fear not; you will no longer live in shame. The shame of your youth and the sorrows of widowhood will be remembered no more, for your Creator will be your husband. The LORD Almighty is his name! He is your Redeemer, the Holy One of Israel, the God of all the earth. For the LORD has called you back from your grief—as though you

were a young wife abandoned by her husband," says your God. "For a brief moment I abandoned you, but with great compassion I will take you back. In a moment of anger I turned my face away for a little while. But with everlasting love I will have compassion on you," says the LORD, your Redeemer.

Reflecting on these verses, express your thanks to God for how He has blessed through this group.

Also, how will you plan to continue to use what you have learned?

Plan of Salvation

How to receive Christ:

1. Admit your need (that you are a sinner).

2. Be willing to turn from your sins (repent).

3. Believe that Jesus Christ died for you on the cross and rose from the grave.

4. Through prayer, invite Jesus Christ to come in and control your life through the Holy Spirit (receive Him as Savior and Lord).

What to Pray

Dear God,
I know that I am a sinner and need Your forgiveness.
I believe that Jesus Christ died for my sins.
I am willing to turn from my sins.
I now invite Jesus Christ to come into my heart and life as my personal Savior.
I am willing, by God's strength, to follow and obey Jesus Christ as the Lord of my life.

_____
Date   Signature

The Bible says: "Everyone who calls on the name of the Lord will be saved" (*Romans 10:13*).

"Yet to all who received him, to those who believed in his name, he gave the right to become children of God" (*John 1:12*).

"Therefore, since we have been justified through faith, we have peace with God through our Lord Jesus Christ" (*Romans 5:1*).

When we receive Christ, we are born into the family of God through the supernatural work of the Holy Spirit, who lives within every believer. This process is called regeneration or the new birth.

Share your decision to receive Christ with another person.

Connect to a local church.

References

Anderson, Neil T. *Victory Over the Darkness*. Ventura, CA: Regal Books, 2000.

Elwell, Walter A. Editor. *Evangelical Dictionary of Theology*. Grand Rapids: Baker Book House, 1984.

Murray, Andrew. *Holy In Christ*. Minneapolis: Bethany Fellowship, no date.

Pearlman, Myer. *Knowing the Doctrines of the Bible*. Springfield, MO: Gospel Publishing House, 1937.

Sande, Ken. *The Peacemaker*. Grand Rapids: Baker Books, 2004.